CONTENTS

Tam: 'Fit d'ye think o' the Gulf situation, Jim?'

Jim: 'Weel, Tam, A think Nick Faldo'll breeze through it.'

War Time 1914-1918

I'm telt ye threw yer watch
Ootower the kirk. The hinmaist
Thing ye did on the wye tae war.
Prood o yon time-piece,
Feart it wad be bladdit.
Did it stop fin it struck the grun?
Yer first watch, Willie, an yer last;
Flung frae ye like yer bairnhood,
In the drapt fit of the mairch past.
Fairm-sodjer-bairn,
In the ower-big uniform
(Onythin dis tae dee in)
Someither-body merriet yer quine,
As the war tae en aa wars
Gaed mairchin ooto mine,
Wi nae hugger-muggery;
The loon fa tint his watch,
Wis blawn tae buggery.

Sheena Blackhall

An Iraqi Student

Quiet spoken Sabbar Sultan in Basra,
I hope you are well as I am unwarlike.
Belligerent Americans are baking
in Arabia, itching to terrify your cities.
May they not, nor you theirs. But shall we ever
resume new-old conclusions about Titus,
Gormenghast, the great flood, Fuchsia, Steerpike?
The walls are higher now, the roads a minefield.
It would be very bad to be forgetful.
One thin line of thought in words, not shifting
as sands are - well, not quite so shifting, language
shifts with anchors dragging - must manage
like a camel-train to make its measured progress
through missile banks, camouflage fatigues, gas-masks
clustered like decapitated insects -
future ruins already lightly dusted
by the desert wind. I hope you tell your students
of this wet green periphery, of reading
Durrell and Bunting, Murdoch and MacDiarmid,
under Gothic - well, not really Gothic - arches;
and commandeered Strathclyde, as missile-haunted
as now the Gulf is, 'The Bunkers of Glen Fruin'
an unwritten skirl, but anyone can hear it.
Keep safe; the edge is everywhere; all know it.

Edwin Morgan

Jerusalem

Sometimes I want to speak;
I want to listen to
Jerusalem. And feel
Sheer light
Touch real thunder
And carry
that brutal cross.

Derek H. Beverley

War Numbers

Kiss your life goodbye,
And bury your troubles in rubble
In the lovely, sunny days
Of vermin and disease.

War 1, 2, 3, 4, 5,

Oh how our selfish grandparents frolicked
Innocently, and had such fun
In the good old days
Of food shortage and destruction

War 6, 7, repeat again 6, 7,

Salvage what is left over
From the latest war
And give it to our children
So they have a war to call their own

War 8, 9, 10   war numbers ... never ending.

Kevin Dolan

Remembrance Day

But for those poppies you'd soon have me fooled
it could be Red Square whilst Joe Stalin drooled
for there are the banners, and there too the guns
Hitler would relish the sight of his sons

Partaking this orgy - this bloodstained parade
which celebrates war lest memories fade.
Our glorious dead, to hell with the rest
and damn their Salvation, whilst here are ours blessed

And blessed by a church which never says kill
yet stands by those weapons and others that will
and equally pure, standing sweet and sublime
the political bastards who'll start it next time.

No, lessons there are from horrors as these
but don't give me uniformed cer'monies please
and don't insult peace from the point of a gun
whilst Dreaming of Glory and battles unwon.

Instead point a finger at why all wars start,
the craze for division, the nationalist art
and ask too the question is this then a cure?
or is it the means by which hatreds endure?

Is this too the lesson those dead souls would want
or is it a callous political front?
and is this the means by which man will unite
or is it a dupe, keeping friends from his sight?

Peter Mearns

Five Children Gunned Down in California

Here there is no uniform,
no generals we can see strutting across fascist yards,
the Annie Jane going down off Vatersay,
the Iolaire sinking off Stornoway,
Patrick Sellar is missing however
though the beautiful green valley is all ablaze
and the cold ruined stances of houses smoulder
in the sweet ashes of the lovely morning light
as it hits the high beauty of Foinavon
and mirrors across the moors of this Mackay country
where I see no military order or Inquisition
or crooked finger calling us to the official front
that besieged the rye grass when I was young
in Uist I remember lying in the Boisdale grass
imagining that Hitler had risen from the dead
and was hiding in the potato fields of Bornish
ready for the assault of the night and could I
cut the telegraph wires before he arrived
at the corner of the field at the edge of the house
where his forgotten shadow suddenly startles this night
the five innocent children who have died again
in the indiscriminate Boisdale of the unordered mind.

Angus Peter Campbell

A Baby Cries Today

A nation of blind or a nation of fools
A nation divided by money and schools
A nation where bullshit is read every day
A nation that's angry but too scared to say!
A nation on Valium is a nation confused
A nation where workers are hated and used
A nation that's scared of the streets late at night
A nation once bright now a very dim light
A nation whose saviours are dead or insane
A nation of nutters in charge of the game
It's a nation I know but can love less and less
It's becoming one terrible mush of a mess!

Derek H. Beverley

War - 3 Haiku

1   Snow shower in springtime
conspicuous
as daffodils in winter

2   Dove flurry
from a howitzer
probable as rabbits from a hat

3   Winter - the world is
a beautiful snowball
tinged blood-red

Keith Murray

Progress

When the world is dead,
and Man is nothing but few,
plant and animal, gone.
When nothing is left,
but a cloud of atomic vapour.

Christopher Hunter (aged 16)

The Sun wis nivvir Dark

The sun wis nivvir dark,
Up in Orkney, sentry-duty,
durin the war,
naebody for miles,
A thocht, A sez te masel,
gey quaet here -
Think er wisnae a war.

Alasdair MacPherson

Two resettings in Scots by Sheena Blackhall of English translations of the T'ang Dynasty Chinese poets, Tu Fu and Li Po, found in A Treasury of Asian Literature, New American Library, editor J.D. Johannan

Nicht in the Biggin bi the Burn

Tu Fu (713-770)

Gloamin sypes doon the Ben
Tae the biggin ayont the dyke.
Bi heich caves
The licht clouds strikk their camp.
The meen rowes ower i' the waves
In the quat at the dowp o a flicht o cranes
The gutsy wolves skirl
As the fears o wartime
Caa the sleep frae men
Fushionless tae command the spheres.

Sheena Blackhall

From **Fighting on the South Frontier**

Li Po (701-762)

There's nae foun tae war.

Ower the killin rigs, the sodgers warssle an dee

Their cuddies belloch their grue tae the lift

Hoodies an kites, reive the intimmers o men

Syne takkin flicht, hing the reid mate ower the airms o
wizzened trees.

Sae are men splytered alang the desert girse

Heid-bummers return teem-neived

Ken ye, the trock o war is hailly evil!

The guidman heists it anely fin hard-caad.

Sheena Blackhall

Christmas Day 1914 France

Pals, real chums,
Germans, Danes, Scots?
It's hard te tell.
Only uniforms appear te change a bloke.
Tak ae time at Christmas when i fechtin stopped
an i men sang te ane anither in i snaw,
"Stille nacht, heilige nacht, alle schläft ...";
drinkin brandy an eatin cake
an jokin as far as translation wid ging.
They taen aff thir helmets an used em as goalposts.
An they watched the sun ging doon, thegither,
on i winter horizon.
Ae day. Ae nicht.
Until i music stopped.
Men like them dinna fash themsels wi
politics an religion.
Thir one weakness wis follyin orders
gien be bummers 'at thrived on thae things.

Keith Murray

The Poppy

The flower of Flanders is red in the blue sky. That blood is still

strong amidst the storm.

That red star is on my calm jacket. The hands are folded and the

eyes are shut.

The potatoes are growing and the roots are so white, the dead

bones among the water and the dew.

And the cows with their helmets and their great horns tasting grass

that was cleansed by them and each skull under the quiet plough

gently fertilising the earth far from heaven.

Iain Crichton Smith

The Dove

You, the dove,
Changing the dark shape of two
In one breath of understanding
Which carries us laughing
From the shore
Where we danced a miniature ballet
On white tips of waves
Reflected heavenwards
In Neptune's silver mirror
To the place
Where we imagined a golden pear tree
And picked the fruits of light
Tossing them gently into the world
For children to catch.

Fiona Cartmell